MINECRAFT™

NEW YORK

Copyright © 2021 by Mojang Synergies AB. MINECRAFT and the Minecraft logo are trademarks of the Microsoft group of companies.

All rights reserved.

Published in the United States by Del Rey, an imprint of Random House, a division of Penguin Random House LLC, New York.

DEL REY is a registered trademark and the CIRCLE colophon is a trademark of Penguin Random House LLC.

Published in hardcover and created in the United Kingdom by Egmont Books UK Limited.

ISBN 978-0-593-15983-5
Ebook ISBN 978-0-593-15984-2

Printed in China on acid-free paper by C & C Offset

Written by Thomas McBrien

Illustrations by Ryan Marsh

randomhousebooks.com

2 4 6 8 9 7 5 3 1

First Edition

Design by John Stuckey

MINECRAFT™
BITE-SIZE
BUILDS

OVER 20 EXCITING MINI-PROJECTS

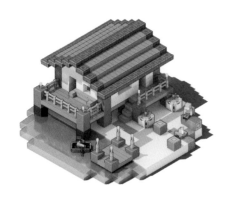

CONTENTS

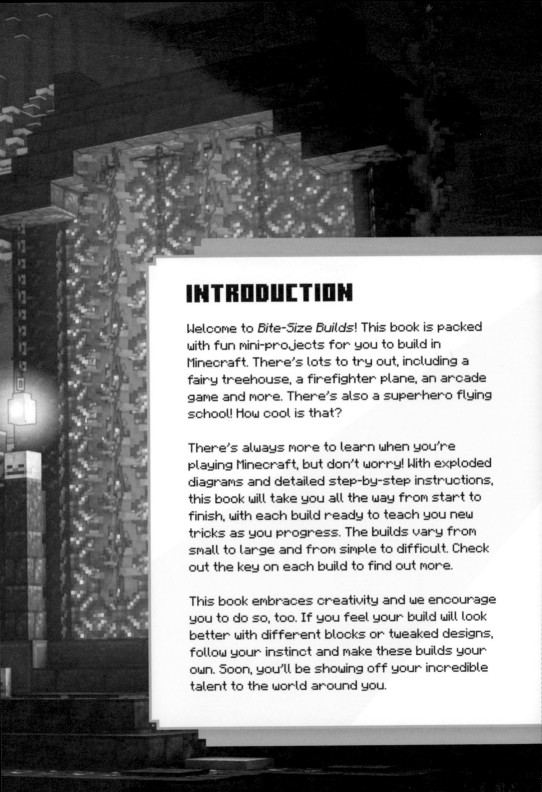

INTRODUCTION

Welcome to *Bite-Size Builds*! This book is packed with fun mini-projects for you to build in Minecraft. There's lots to try out, including a fairy treehouse, a firefighter plane, an arcade game and more. There's also a superhero flying school! How cool is that?

There's always more to learn when you're playing Minecraft, but don't worry! With exploded diagrams and detailed step-by-step instructions, this book will take you all the way from start to finish, with each build ready to teach you new tricks as you progress. The builds vary from small to large and from simple to difficult. Check out the key on each build to find out more.

This book embraces creativity and we encourage you to do so, too. If you feel your build will look better with different blocks or tweaked designs, follow your instinct and make these builds your own. Soon, you'll be showing off your incredible talent to the world around you.

GENERAL BUILD TIPS

The builds in this book are suitable for both beginners and experts. Whether you're a first-time player or a seasoned Minecrafter, we've included a few general build tips to help ensure you have a great time following the guides and completing the builds.

CREATIVE MODE

Complete the builds in Creative mode. With unlimited access to all the blocks in the game and instant block removal, Creative mode is the easiest way to build in Minecraft. If you like a challenge, each structure can be built in Survival mode – but be warned! It will take a lot more time and preparation.

BUILD PREPARATION

Before starting a build, take a moment to look at the instructions and consider where you want to place the build and how much space you will need to complete it. Give yourself plenty of space to work.

TEMPORARY BLOCKS

Temporary building blocks are helpful for counting out spaces and placing floating items. Using temporary blocks will also help you with tricky block placement.

Count the dimensions using different color blocks. This row represents 13 blocks.

Use temporary blocks to help place floating blocks.

HOTBARS

Most builds use lots of different blocks. You can prepare your blocks in the hotbar before starting for quick access, and if you don't have enough space, you can save up to nine hotbars in the inventory window.

BLOCK PLACEMENT

Placing a block beside an interactive one, such as an enchanting table, can be tricky. By clicking to place down the block, you'll interact with the interactive one instead. In order to place a block without interacting, first crouch and then click to place it.

CREEPER IN THE WOODS

You can build lots of impressive structures with basic shapes. This build will show you how to create a classic mob, the creeper, using a combination of square and rectangular shapes. Get ready to show invading mobs that you're not afraid of them!

DIFFICULTY:

★☆☆☆☆

🕒 20 mins

BUILD TIP

Use temporary blocks to join the feet and body together. Remove these blocks when you're done.

5 blocks
5 blocks
Gray concrete
3 blocks
7 blocks
5 blocks
Green concrete powder
White concrete
Lime terracotta
Green terracotta
4 blocks
Green concrete
5 blocks
3 blocks

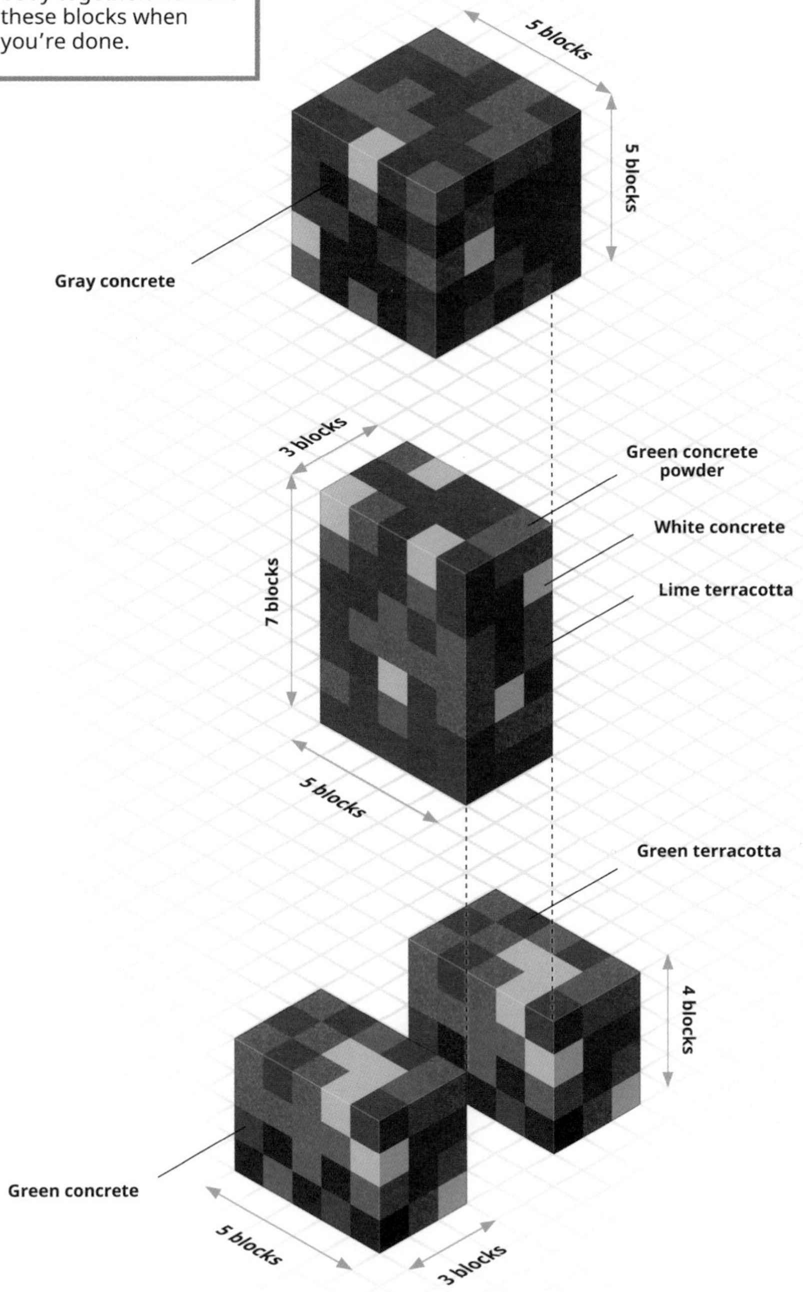

TOADSTOOL HOUSE

There's nothing quite as magical as a toadstool house set on the edge of an old, forgotten forest. With bees, mushrooms and even a witch's hut nearby, this home has everything you need for a perfect fairy-tale adventure.

DIFFICULTY:
★★☆☆☆
🕐 35 mins

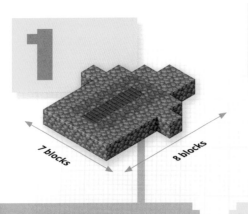

1

Start by creating the foundation for the toadstool house using cobblestone, mossy cobblestone and spruce planks. The cobblestone is the outline for the house.

7 blocks

8 blocks

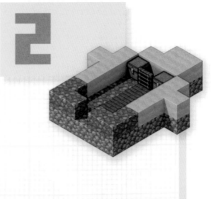

2

Begin building the walls up from the edge of the foundation using mossy cobblestone and mushroom stems. Place a trapdoor on the ground and open it; then, while crouching, place a ladder against it. Add two chests.

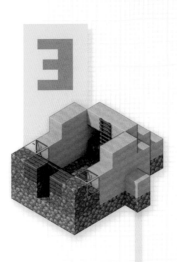

3

Continue building the walls using mossy cobblestone, mushroom stems, spruce planks and glass blocks. Extend the ladder with two more oak trapdoors and ladders, and put an oak door in the doorway.

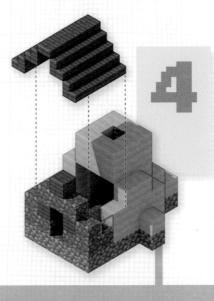

4

Place three mossy cobblestone and a spruce plank above the doorway and then create a roof using oak stairs and oak slabs, as shown. Continue building the toadstool's stem with two 3x3 mushroom stem rings and extend the ladder up through the toadstool's stem.

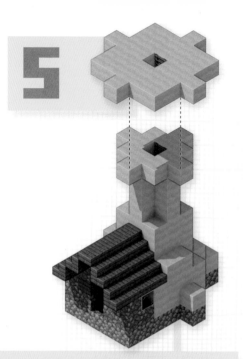

5

Continue building the next five layers of the toadstool's stem. The top two layers are larger to create the toadstool cap shape. Extend the ladder up through the toadstool's stem again.

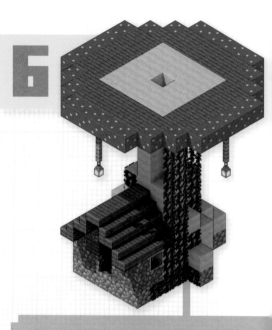

6

Start building the toadstool cap with a 5x5 layer of mushroom stem, spruce planks and red mushroom blocks as shown. Hang lanterns with spruce fences, and add vines down the toadstool's stem.

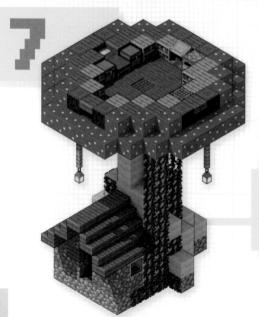

7

Get creative and decorate the interiors. This room has a bed, storage and a lectern for recording adventures.

Add a ring of red mushroom blocks, spruce logs and spruce slabs around the cap. Extend the ladder to the top floor and place a spruce trapdoor above it.

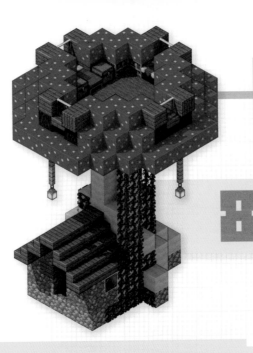

Build a window on each side of the toadstool cap using two spruce planks, a glass pane and a spruce trapdoor. Then connect each of the windows with zigzagging red mushroom blocks, giving the toadstool cap a round shape.

8

9

Add roofs above each of the windows using spruce stairs and spruce slabs. Then use more red mushroom blocks to connect each of the roofs.

10

Finally, complete the toadstool cap with another ring of red mushroom blocks and a 3x3 red mushroom roof above it. Your toadstool house is now ready for an adventure!

TROPICAL BEACH CHALET

The beach is where memories are made and woes are forgotten. This one-room chalet is the perfect getaway, with fishing, swimming and campfire cooking all packed into one fun spot. This beachfront home even has a private dock and ocean-view veranda.

DIFFICULTY:
★★★☆☆
🕑 25 mins

14

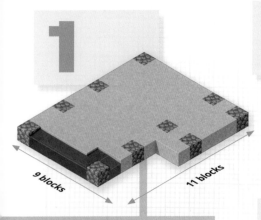

1 Find a nice beach by the ocean and start building a base for the beachfront chalet using cobblestone and sand. If the water is deep, extend the cobblestone to reach the seabed.

9 blocks

11 blocks

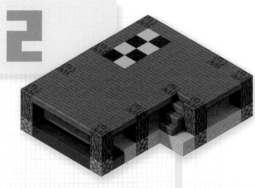

2 Begin raising the chalet above ground with ten 2-block-tall oak wood columns. Then add a floor using acacia slabs. In the back corner, create a tiled kitchen area with gray and white concrete. Finally, add acacia stairs leading up to the entrance.

Create a bench using 3 birch stairs.

Use activator rails, furnaces and quartz stairs to create special stoves.

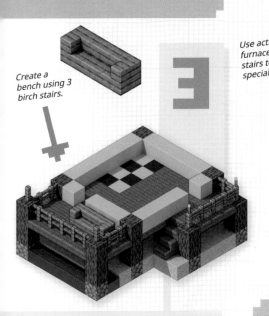

3 Start building the walls with white concrete and oak wood. Then add a railing using oak wood and oak fences. Place two torches by the entrance as shown.

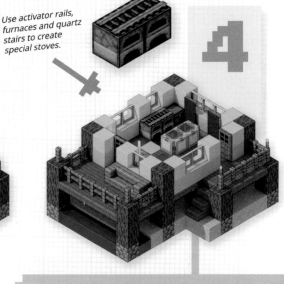

4 Extend the walls using smooth quartz, oak wood and glass panes. Create custom-made stoves for the kitchen, and add oak doors. Decorate the room with banners, beds and a chest.

5

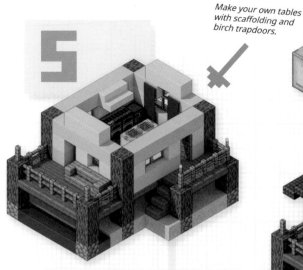

Make your own tables with scaffolding and birch trapdoors.

6

Continue to extend the walls using oak wood and white concrete, and place three smooth quartz in the center of the front and rear walls to support the roof. Add a few tables to the kitchen.

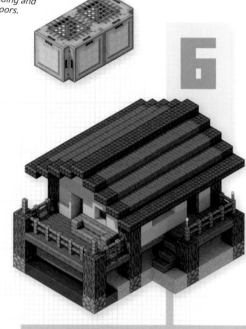

Build a roof for the chalet using dark prismarine and acacia slabs. Create the dark prismarine slab outline first, then complete the roof with cascading acacia slabs.

7

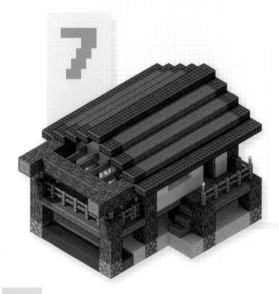

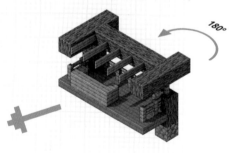

180°

Add a pergola to the chalet by creating an H-shaped structure above the veranda using oak wood. Then add slats to the pergola using oak signs.

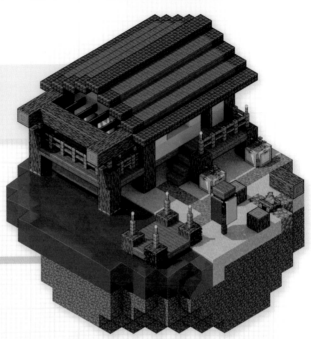

Add a gravel path leading up to the entrance, and create flower beds with birch trapdoors and dirt. Finally, build the chalet essentials, then sit back and enjoy the sea breeze!

CHALET ESSENTIALS

A beachfront chalet is not complete without a dock and campfire. And if you're swimming, you're going to need a towel rack, too. Complete your chalet with these final additions.

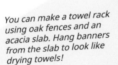

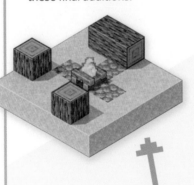

You can make a towel rack using oak fences and an acacia slab. Hang banners from the slab to look like drying towels!

Build a dock by the water using oak wood and acacia slabs. Light it up with torches so you can always find it, day or night.

Design a cozy outdoor area with cobblestone, a campfire and oak wood. Place the oak wood blocks both upright and lying down to make them stand out.

ALARM SYSTEM

You can protect your base from mobs with walls and traps, but how do you stop a cunning player? With an alarm system, of course! This build will show you how to use a simple redstone mechanism to keep your valuables safe from unwanted visitors.

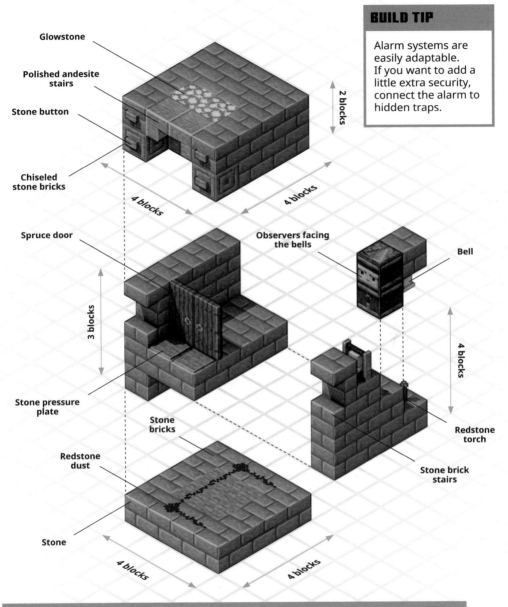

Glowstone

Polished andesite stairs

Stone button

Chiseled stone bricks

4 blocks

4 blocks

2 blocks

BUILD TIP

Alarm systems are easily adaptable. If you want to add a little extra security, connect the alarm to hidden traps.

Spruce door

Observers facing the bells

Bell

3 blocks

4 blocks

Stone pressure plate

Stone bricks

Redstone dust

Redstone torch

Stone

Stone brick stairs

4 blocks

4 blocks

REDSTONE MECHANISM

This alarm system uses a simple redstone circuit to activate the bells. The pressure plates in the doorway are connected to the redstone torch that activates the bells. When a player steps on the pressure plate, the bells will ring to announce their presence.

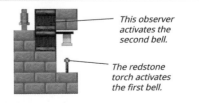

This observer activates the second bell.

The redstone torch activates the first bell.

SURVIVALIST'S VAULT

With hundreds of different blocks and items available in Minecraft, it's no surprise that storage chests can get a little disorganized. This underground vault build is a great addition to any Survival base, helping you find the blocks you need in an instant.

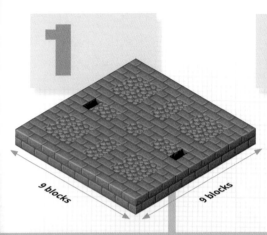

1

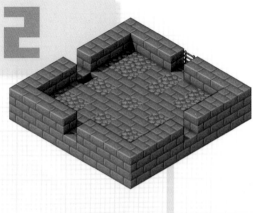

2

Start by digging a trench 9 blocks deep and excavate a 9x9 area for the foundation, as shown. Create the foundations for the vault at the bottom of the cavern using cobblestone, cobblestone stairs and stone bricks.

Begin building the walls around the edges of the foundation. Leave a gap in the center of each wall and place a ladder in one of the remaining block spaces.

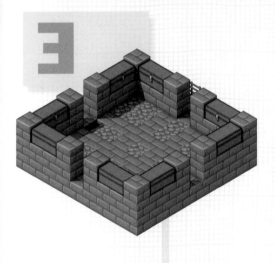

3

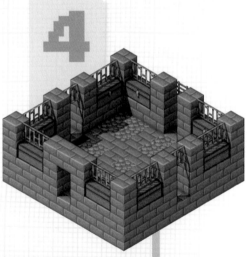

4

Place eight large chests around the room, so there are two on each side. Add stone bricks on either side and another ladder above the one already placed.

Add another layer to the walls using stone bricks and iron bars, which should be added over all the chests and two of the wall gaps. Place an upside-down stone brick stairs block in the entrance.

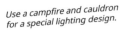

5

Use a campfire and cauldron for a special lighting design.

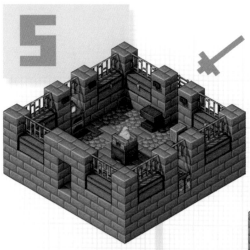

Add details to the interior with polished blackstone buttons, lanterns and utility blocks. This vault has an anvil, grindstone, furnace and crafting table.

6

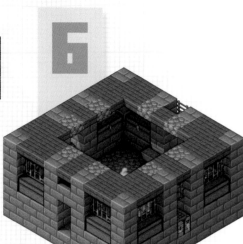

Create a second-floor balcony using stone bricks, spruce slabs and cobblestone stairs to increase the vault's storage capacity. Extend the ladder to reach the new balcony.

7

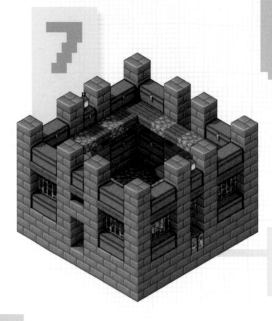

Add two more stone brick layers to the walls. Then place eight more large chests in the gaps, with an extra chest and lantern in each alcove.

Create a banister around the balcony using spruce trapdoors.

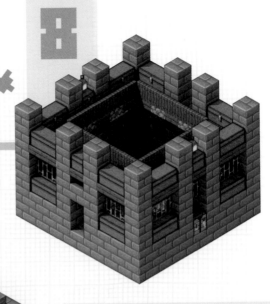

Add a final layer of stone bricks to the vault walls and then seal the top of the vault with a stone roof.

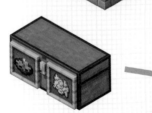

Finally, fill your chests with stores of blocks and items. Place frames on each of the chests and fill them with items to represent the contents of the chest. You will never struggle to find your items again!

23

COMBINATION LOCK

A vault is an excellent way to keep all your valuables well organized; however, it also makes a juicy target for raiding intruders. This build will teach you a special redstone combination lock that will add an extra layer of security to your vault.

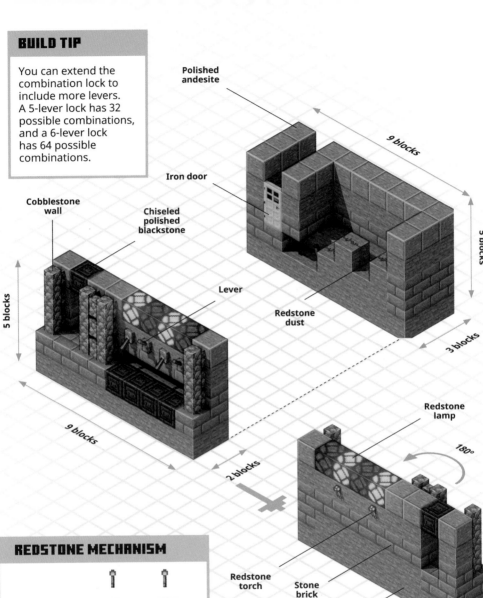

BUILD TIP

You can extend the combination lock to include more levers. A 5-lever lock has 32 possible combinations, and a 6-lever lock has 64 possible combinations.

Polished andesite

9 blocks

5 blocks

3 blocks

Iron door

Cobblestone wall

Chiseled polished blackstone

5 blocks

Lever

Redstone dust

9 blocks

2 blocks

Redstone lamp

180°

REDSTONE MECHANISM

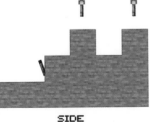

SIDE

TOP

Redstone torch

Stone brick

Stone

This combination lock uses redstone torches, redstone dust and stone blocks to create "notches" for a combination lock. To set the code, simply add or move a redstone torch and the stone block beneath it. This redstone mechanism is called an "AND" gate.

FAIRY TREEHOUSE

The biggest challenge of building in forested biomes is clearing away trees and foliage to fit all your structures. But there are creative solutions! Building above ground has its perks, like keeping you safe from roaming zombies. This build is all about using trees to your advantage.

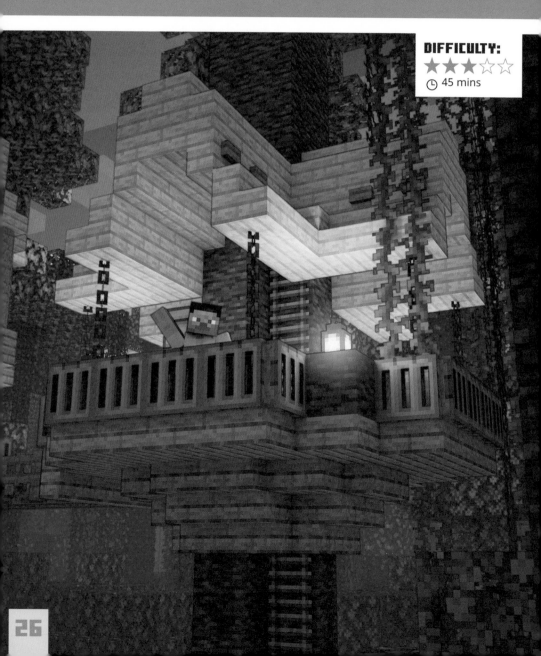

1

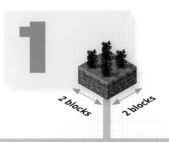

2 blocks · 2 blocks

Create a giant tree by placing jungle saplings in a 2x2 square on grass blocks and growing them using bone meal. You could also use spruce saplings.

2

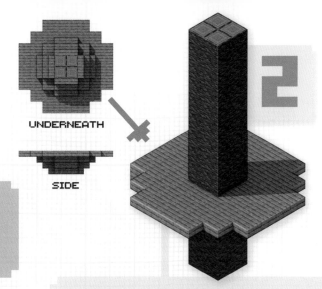

UNDERNEATH

SIDE

Build a platform around the tree using jungle slabs and jungle stairs. The platform should be four blocks above ground level.

3

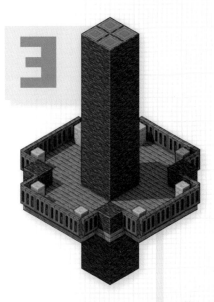

Add an acacia trapdoor banister around the platform. Then place four jungle wood blocks and eight sandstone walls on the platform as shown.

4

Create ambient lighting for the treehouse with soul lanterns.

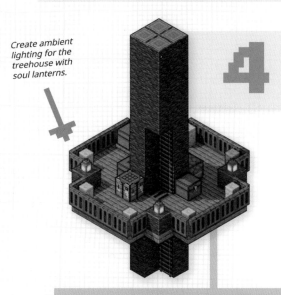

Create an entrance to the treehouse by removing nine blocks from the tree trunk. Place ladders leading up into the treehouse, and add an acacia trapdoor to close the platform.

5

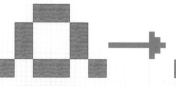

TEMPORARY
OUTLINE

STAIR
BLOCKS

Add a roof above the platform using birch stairs. Start by creating an outline for the roof using temporary blocks, then place the stair blocks as shown.

6

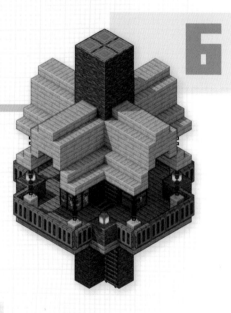

Repeat the roof structure on all four sides of the trunk until the platform is completely covered.

7

Join the roof to the sandstone with chains and add detail to the roof with acacia buttons. Finally, complete the treehouse with some vines against the tree trunk.

TREEHOUSE EXTENSION

Need more space? You can create a second giant tree and build a bridge between the two treehouses. You can even make the second treehouse larger with an additional platform!

Build another treehouse and join them together with an acacia gate and campfire bridge. Simply link the two trees with campfires and extinguish the fires with a shovel.

Create platforms using the instructions in steps 2 and 3. Why not fill your new platform with useful tools, like an enchanting table, anvil and grindstone?

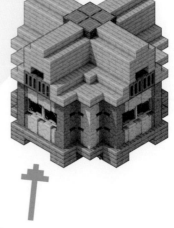

Give the new treehouse a second floor with a fresh look. Use glass, sandstone and red sandstone to create a sheltered room at the top of the tree.

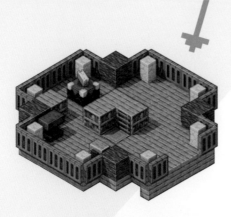

SUPERHERO FLYING SCHOOL

As all superheroes know, the fastest way to catch the villain is by flying. This floating island build will teach you everything you need to know to soar across the skies. Beginners can jump off the launch board to get started, while experts can line up for a turn on the elytra launcher.

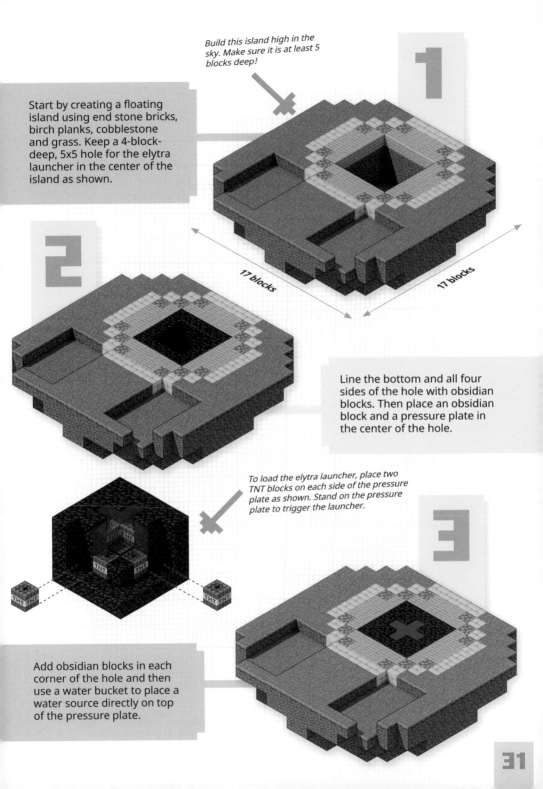

Start by creating a floating island using end stone bricks, birch planks, cobblestone and grass. Keep a 4-block-deep, 5x5 hole for the elytra launcher in the center of the island as shown.

Build this island high in the sky. Make sure it is at least 5 blocks deep!

17 blocks

17 blocks

Line the bottom and all four sides of the hole with obsidian blocks. Then place an obsidian block and a pressure plate in the center of the hole.

To load the elytra launcher, place two TNT blocks on each side of the pressure plate as shown. Stand on the pressure plate to trigger the launcher.

Add obsidian blocks in each corner of the hole and then use a water bucket to place a water source directly on top of the pressure plate.

31

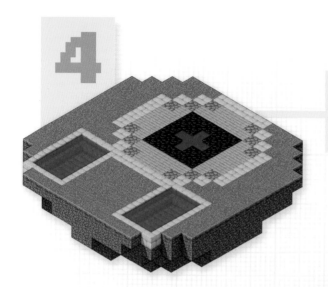

4

Create two landing pools using end stone stairs and bricks and fill them with water. These pools will ensure a safe landing after every flight.

5

Next, start building the marquee that covers the elytra launcher. Build supporting pillars using end stone walls and birch fences.

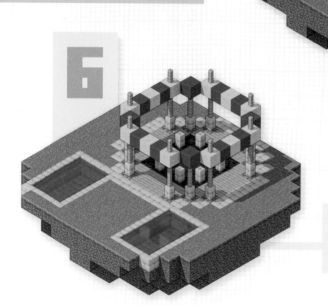

6

Start adding a roof to the marquee with a ring of red and white wool. Then place birch fences in the corners as shown.

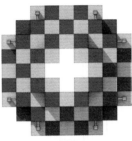

TOP

SIDE

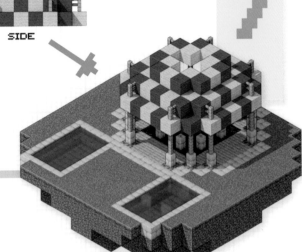

Add another two rings to the marquee roof using red and white wool, leaving an X-shaped gap above the elytra launcher.

Create a walkway leading up to the marquee using end stone bricks, end stone walls and birch planks. Then create the jumping board with birch slabs.

Place a chest in the marquee and fill it with elytras and TNT!

Finally, complete the flying school with a ring of large ferns around the floating island, and light the walkway with lanterns. Then grab some fireworks, equip an elytra and start flying!

FLY LIKE A SUPERHERO

Now that your flying school is all set up, it's time to learn how to fly!
Follow these simple steps to get started. Remember, practice makes
perfect, so keep trying until you're flying around like a superhero.

1 First, put on your wings – equip an elytra in your chestplate slot! Elytras are rare wings found only in End ships. They are essential for flying in Minecraft.

2 Now it's time to fly. Step up to the launch board and when you're ready, dive! Once you're in the sky, press the jump key to start gliding on the elytra.

3 Next, fill your off-hand with a stack of fireworks. When you're flying, shoot the fireworks to gain momentum as you soar across the sky. Once you're a proficient flyer, have a turn in the elytra launcher!

LOADING YOUR LAUNCHER

When chasing down villains, speed is of the essence!
An elytra launcher is the fastest way to start flying.
Simply load the launcher, step onto the pressure plate
and brace yourself for blast-off!

1 Load the launcher with eight TNT. First, place four TNT at the bottom of the launcher, then stack four more TNT on top of them.

2 Step into the launcher and stand directly on top of the pressure plate.

TNT will detonate after 4 seconds!

3 Wait for the TNT to detonate and launch you into the air. Once in the air, tap the jump key to start flying. Keep an eye on your health bar if you're playing Survival mode.

ITEM DESTROYER

You may have a large vault to store all the treasures you find, but what about all the trash that's weighing you down? This redstone mechanism is a great tool for destroying blocks you don't want: simply pop them in the chest and watch as they disappear.

DIFFICULTY:
★☆☆☆☆
🕒 5 mins

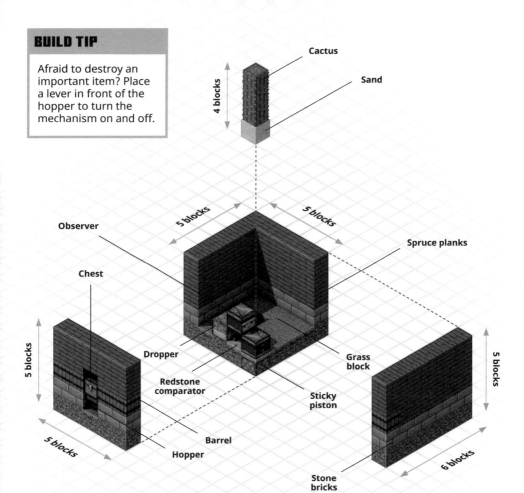

Cactus

Sand

4 blocks

Observer

Chest

Spruce planks

5 blocks

5 blocks

5 blocks

5 blocks

Dropper

Redstone comparator

Grass block

Sticky piston

Barrel

Hopper

Stone bricks

6 blocks

REDSTONE MECHANISM

This item destroyer shoots the unwanted blocks in the chest out from a dispenser and into a cactus. Each item destroyed activates the redstone comparator, which ensures that all items are gradually removed from the chest.

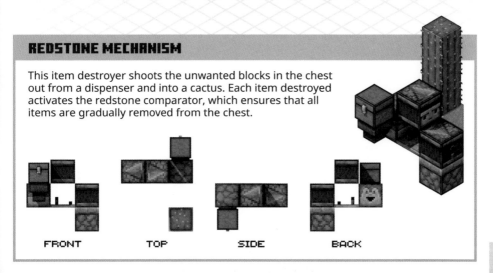

FRONT

TOP

SIDE

BACK

37

FIREFIGHTER PLANE

By combining slime blocks, pistons and a variety of redstone components, you can create your very own moving vehicle. This firefighter plane will speed you in a straight line toward your destination. Make sure to pack a full stack of redstone torches — you're going to need them!

1

Build a temporary cobblestone pillar to lift the plane off the ground and into the sky. Then place an observer facing the cobblestone.

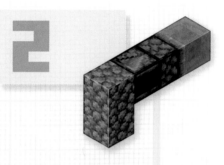

2

Place a sticky piston facing away from the observer. Then add a slime block.

3

Add four more slime blocks around the observer and sticky piston. The slime blocks will hold your plane together as you add more blocks.

4

Remove the temporary cobblestone pillar and add three more slime blocks in front of the sticky piston.

The three pistons provide
the pushing and pulling
that transports the plane.

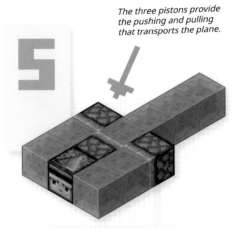

Place two more sticky pistons facing
the slime as shown.

Then add two more observers
facing away from the sticky pistons.

Sticky pistons have a
12-block push limit. Don't
add any extra blocks or the
plane may not work.

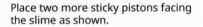

7

You could also
camouflage the
plane by using lime
and green carpets!

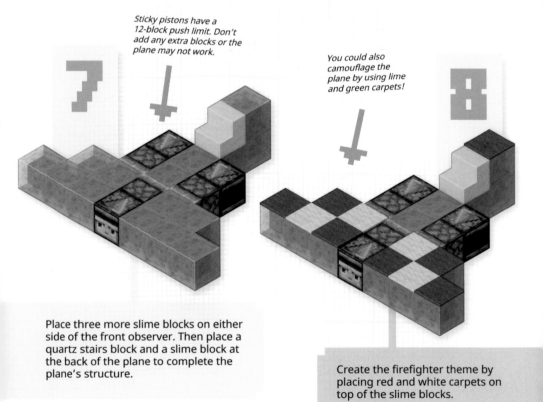

8

Place three more slime blocks on either
side of the front observer. Then place a
quartz stairs block and a slime block at
the back of the plane to complete the
plane's structure.

Create the firefighter theme by
placing red and white carpets on
top of the slime blocks.

9

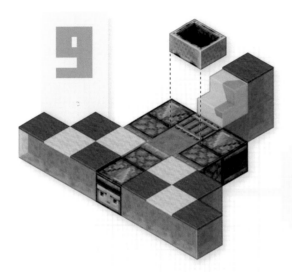

Finally, add a passenger seat using a rail and cart as shown. Sit in the cart when traveling to avoid falling out!

HOW DOES IT WORK?

To start the plane, place a redstone torch on top of the front observer.

To stop the plane, move the redstone torch on top of the slime.

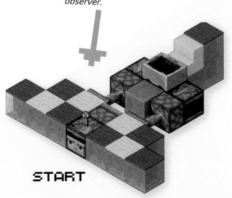

START

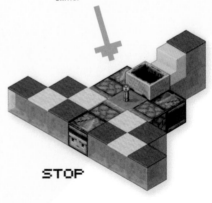

STOP

SHOOTING GALLERY

This exciting minigame will test your accuracy with a bow and arrow, hurling eggs, or even splash potions! It has a clever vertical redstone transmission system that you might find useful when creating other redstone mechanisms. Invite your friends to come and play to see which of you is the best shot!

1

9 blocks

5 blocks

Start by finding a flat, open area for the arcade game and select a suitable spot to build your first target. Then create the base for the target's redstone mechanism using grass and lime terracotta blocks.

2

Place a target block in front of the lime terracotta and create a redstone signal behind it using redstone dust.

When hit by a projectile, the target block will send a signal through the redstone dust to light up the redstone lamp.

3

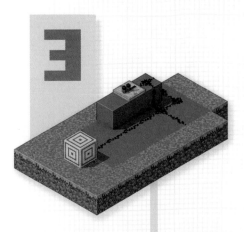

Place three lime terracotta blocks in a row with a redstone repeater on the center block. Then connect the redstone repeater to the target block with another redstone dust.

4

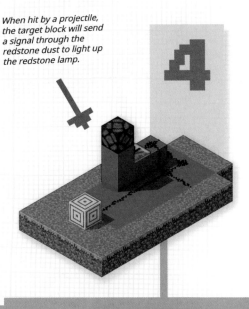

Next, link the target block to a raised light signal by adding another terracotta block with a redstone lamp placed on top of it.

Place three more lime terracotta blocks and extend the redstone signal with two more redstone dust.

Add a second raised light signal using another lime terracotta block and another redstone lamp.

The number of redstone lamps that light up will depend on the accuracy of your shot. Invite a friend and take turns shooting to see who has the best aim!

Build a third and final light signal for the target using another redstone lamp and more lime terracotta blocks. Join the redstone signal to the redstone lamp with another redstone dust.

Your minigame can have as many targets as you like! Simply repeat steps 1 to 8 to create multiple targets.

Finally, disguise the target's redstone mechanism with grass blocks so that visitors can only guess how you created this fun game. You can increase your minigame's difficulty by creating multiple targets.

MINIGAME SETUP

It's time to create your minigame! Build your desired number of targets, placed equal distance apart, and create a platform to shoot from. This shooting gallery has three targets to aim at.

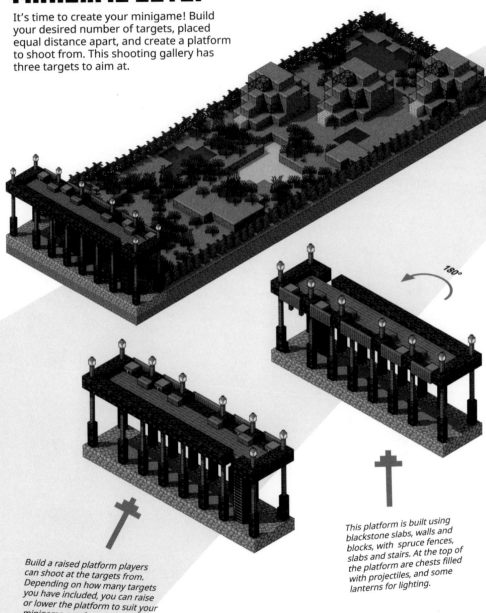

180°

Build a raised platform players can shoot at the targets from. Depending on how many targets you have included, you can raise or lower the platform to suit your minigame needs.

This platform is built using blackstone slabs, walls and blocks, with spruce fences, slabs and stairs. At the top of the platform are chests filled with projectiles, and some lanterns for lighting.

HALLOWEEN MAZE

Mazes are fun and easy projects, and they are endlessly adaptable to fit
your ideas. You can design a maze by laying out a twisting, winding pattern
on the ground, then adding a few dead ends and small traps to catch
players unaware. Make sure there's only one way in and one way out!

DIFFICULTY:
★★★☆☆
🕐 30 mins

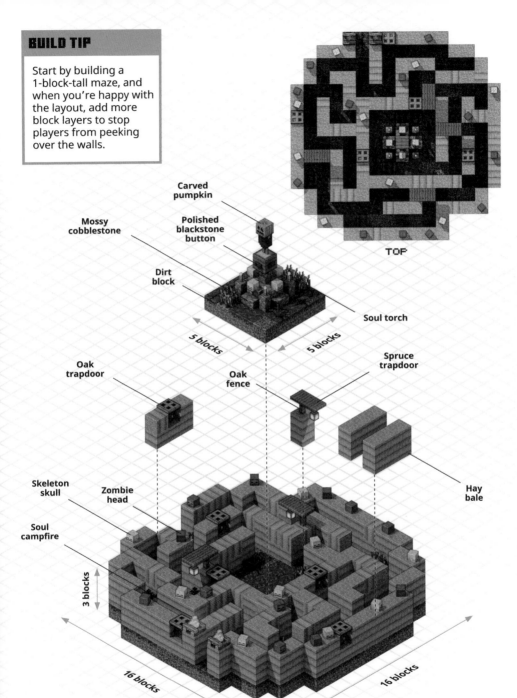

Carved pumpkin

Mossy cobblestone

Polished blackstone button

Dirt block

Soul torch

TOP

5 blocks

5 blocks

Oak trapdoor

Oak fence

Spruce trapdoor

Hay bale

Skeleton skull

Zombie head

Soul campfire

3 blocks

16 blocks

16 blocks

47

TRAIN STATION

Transport is an essential element of Minecraft. Whether you're building a large modern city or a small farming town, you may want to create your own railway system for getting around. Building a railway system is easy with this simple two-track station.

Start by creating the foundation of your train station and its first platform using stone bricks, stone brick slabs, andesite, polished andesite, smooth quartz and jungle planks.

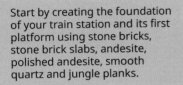

1

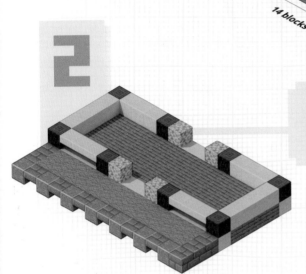

14 blocks

9 blocks

2

Begin building the station walls using spruce wood, diorite, smooth quartz and upside-down smooth quartz stairs.

This ticket barrier is made using an iron trapdoor, quartz and stone button. The diorite is to stop passengers sneaking in!

3

Add a ticket barrier by the station entrance. Then create spruce stair benches around the interior for passengers. Use two spruce stairs next to each other to make longer benches.

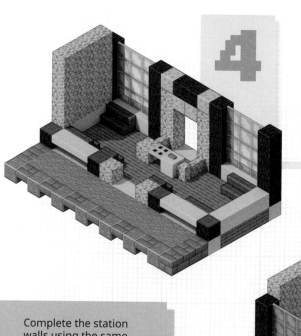

4

Create an archway above the entrance and continue building the station walls using diorite, polished andesite, spruce wood and yellow stained glass panes.

5

Complete the station walls using the same blocks. Then place iron bars above the ticket barrier and hang lanterns to light up the station.

6

Add a roof to the station building. Place a row of jungle planks atop both of the long walls and then complete the roof using jungle slabs.

Add some outdoor lighting by placing stone brick stairs at the top of each spruce column and hanging lanterns from iron bars. Then put two dark oak doors and two dark oak trapdoors in each entryway.

7

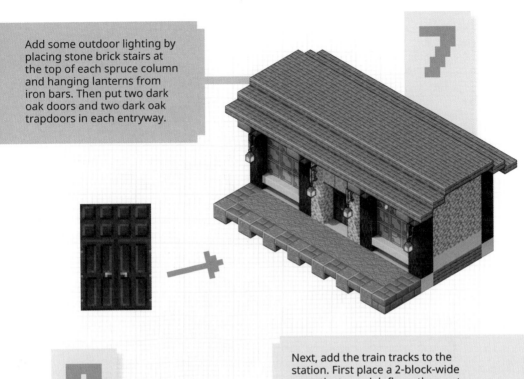

8

Next, add the train tracks to the station. First place a 2-block-wide smooth stone slab floor, then put rails on both sides of the slabs. Add a powered rail and redstone torch at one end of the track, and an activator rail and bell at the opposite end.

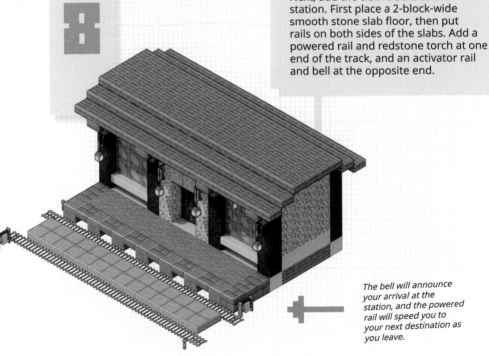

The bell will announce your arrival at the station, and the powered rail will speed you to your next destination as you leave.

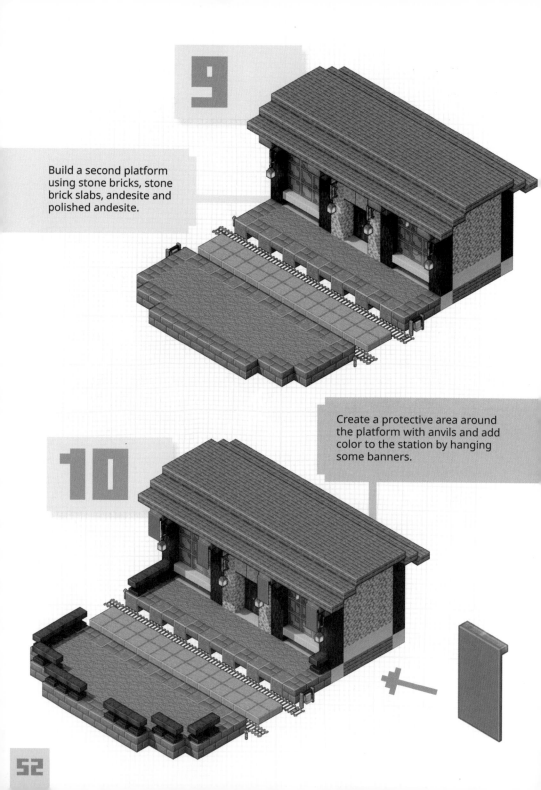

9

Build a second platform using stone bricks, stone brick slabs, andesite and polished andesite.

10

Create a protective area around the platform with anvils and add color to the station by hanging some banners.

PLATFORM EXTRAS

Your train station is not yet finished!
Complete the platform with some
extra features. Lighting is essential
for passenger security and this
cool bridge will help them cross the
tracks safely.

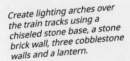

Join the two platforms
together with a bridge.
Use spruce stairs and
spruce slabs to connect
the platforms, then
create a handrail by
lining the bridge with
jungle trapdoors.

Create lighting arches over
the train tracks using a
chiseled stone base, a stone
brick wall, three cobblestone
walls and a lantern.

Decorate the platform with
a special flowerpot made of
spruce trapdoors, dirt and
rosebushes. You can also
add more seating for your
passengers.

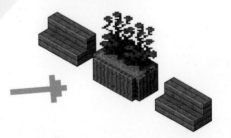

CART COLLECTOR

As you begin to venture to new areas, your railway lines will become more and more intricate. Cart collectors are an excellent way to manage your carts. To begin your journey, simply open the chest, grab a cart and place it on the rails. When you arrive at your destination, the cart will automatically be collected and returned to the chest.

DIFFICULTY:
★★☆☆☆
🕐 10 mins

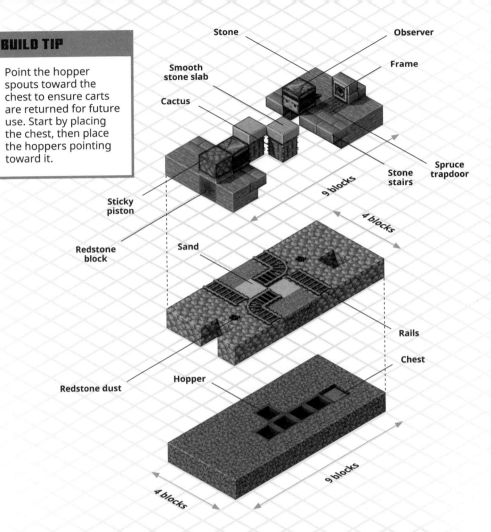

BUILD TIP

Point the hopper spouts toward the chest to ensure carts are returned for future use. Start by placing the chest, then place the hoppers pointing toward it.

Stone

Observer

Smooth stone slab

Frame

Cactus

Stone stairs

Spruce trapdoor

Sticky piston

Redstone block

Sand

Rails

Chest

Redstone dust

Hopper

9 blocks

4 blocks

4 blocks

9 blocks

REDSTONE MECHANISM

This cart collector rushes carts into cacti to be destroyed. The carts are then collected by the hoppers and transported to the chest. Make sure the hoppers are pointing in the right direction!

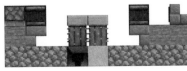

HOPPERS

SIDE

SIDE

TOP

BOUNCY CASTLE

Many of the blocks in Minecraft have special properties that can be used to create some unique structures. Built using slime blocks, carpets and banners, this colorful castle is not exactly as it seems. The bouncy floors will make a tour of the grounds much more fun than visitors expected!

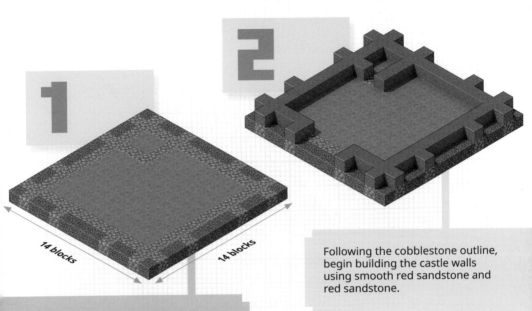

Start by laying the foundations for the bouncy castle using dirt, slime and cobblestone. The cobblestone will be the outline for the bouncy castle.

Following the cobblestone outline, begin building the castle walls using smooth red sandstone and red sandstone.

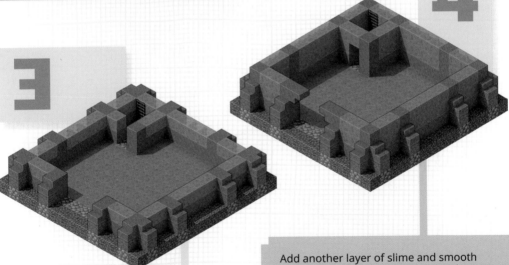

Continue building the walls using smooth red sandstone, smooth red sandstone stairs and slime. Then place ladders in the back corner to climb the castle tower.

Add another layer of slime and smooth red sandstone to the walls. Then, above the entrance, place two upside-down smooth red sandstone stairs to create an archway.

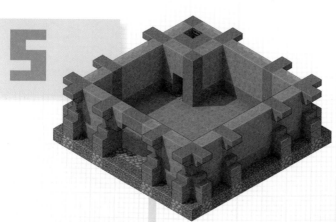

5

Continue the slime and smooth red sandstone walls another layer higher, then place upside-down smooth red sandstone stairs around the exterior. Build a red sandstone slab floor at the top of the tower.

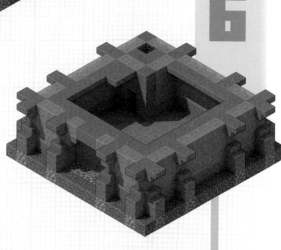

6

Create a walkway around the castle walls using upside-down red sandstone stairs and a red sandstone slab.

7

Next, build a defensive walkway, known as a rampart, around the castle using red sandstone and its walls and stairs variants.

Continue building the castle tower with four more layers of smooth red sandstone and slime. Then place red sandstone walls along the rampart.

9

Extend the ladder to the top of the tower and build another red sandstone slab floor. Place two upside-down smooth red sandstone stairs in each corner of the tower, and create a jumping platform using smooth red sandstone slabs.

This bouncy castle uses a yellow and light blue checkered pattern with soul lanterns for a playful theme.

10

Finally, add a barrier around the top of the tower with red sandstone, red sandstone walls and upside-down smooth red sandstone stairs. Then decorate your bouncy castle with carpets and banners for when the fun begins!

MEDIEVAL WINDMILL

Often the best projects start with down-to-earth ideas. There's no structure more down-to-earth than the humble windmill, an industrious building used to mill wheat into flour. The simple stone bricks and rudimentary woods give this project a distinct medieval flavor.

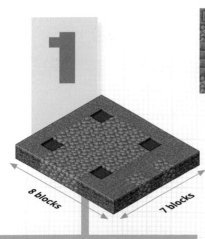

BACK WALL

Start by laying the foundation for the windmill using grass, cobblestone and water as shown. The cobblestone will be the base of the windmill.

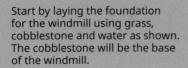

8 blocks

7 blocks

Using cobblestone, stone bricks, chiseled stone bricks and polished diorite, build the four walls of the windmill. Give the windmill some natural light with a spruce fence gate window on each of the back walls.

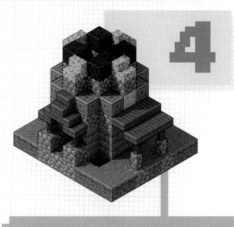

Add a roof above the entrance using spruce stairs, fences and slabs, then place a spruce door in the doorway. Then create an awning on the side wall with spruce slabs, spruce fences and cobblestone walls.

Continue building the next two layers of the walls. First place a layer of diagonally placed cobblestone in a diamond shape; then, on top of the cobblestone, place alternating spruce wood and diorite stairs.

ROOF

5

Build three more layers of the walls using spruce wood, diorite and polished diorite, with three spruce fence gate windows on the top layer. Then add two more diorite and spruce wood layers, with three spruce wood on top.

6

Create a roof for the windmill using cobblestone slabs and spruce stairs. Start by placing a row of cobblestone slabs at the top of the windmill, then add two rows of spruce stairs on either side as shown.

7

Next, create a spruce wood beam to support the windmill vanes. The beam sticks out of the windmill below the roof and has spruce wood blocks sticking out in four directions.

8

Create the first vane using three spruce wood, three spruce fences and four white wool as shown.

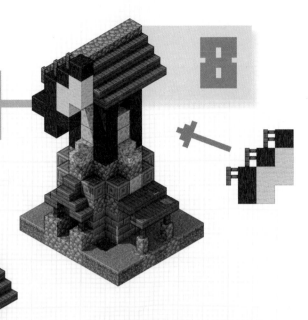

9

Create another three vanes as in the last step, each vane rotating around the spruce wood beam.

10

This windmill will look fantastic built among wheat fields!

Finally, complete the windmill with some finishing details. Place spruce and stone buttons on the vanes and hang spruce fences from the roof corners. Now plant wheat farms around the windmill!

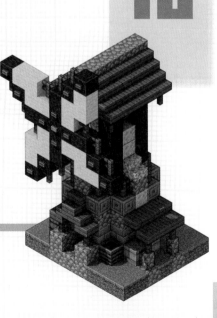

PORTAL TOGGLE

The Nether is a dangerous place filled with dangerous mobs. You can visit by building a portal, but watch out! Unguarded portals are an open invitation for roaming mobs. Protect yourself, and the Overworld, by equipping your portal with an on-off toggle.

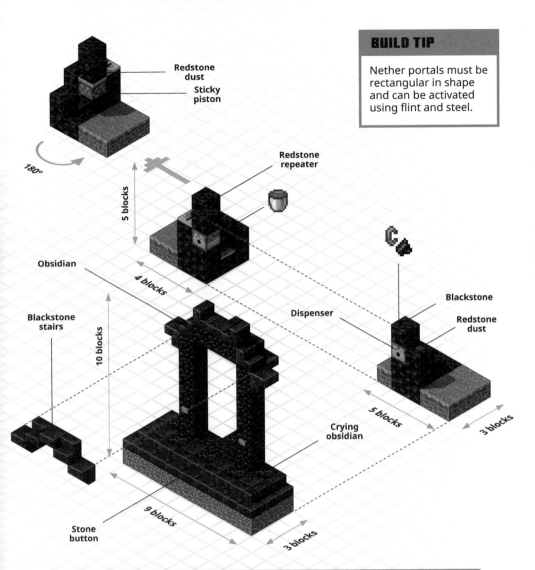

Redstone dust

Sticky piston

180°

5 blocks

Redstone repeater

Obsidian

4 blocks

Blackstone

Dispenser

Blackstone stairs

10 blocks

Redstone dust

Crying obsidian

5 blocks

3 blocks

9 blocks

3 blocks

Stone button

REDSTONE MECHANISM

This portal toggle is controlled by the two dispensers containing a flint and steel, and a water bucket. The dispenser on the right-hand side contains a water bucket and is connected to a redstone repeater. The repeater will ensure the portal deactivates without the water flooding everywhere.

TOP

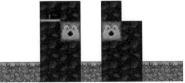

FRONT

OUTDOOR AMPHITHEATER

Hosting a talent show for all your friends? An outdoor amphitheater will provide you with the perfect venue for showcasing their talents! This ancient-style build features some complicated round structures that will give you a real challenge.

DIFFICULTY:
★★★☆☆
🕐 30 mins

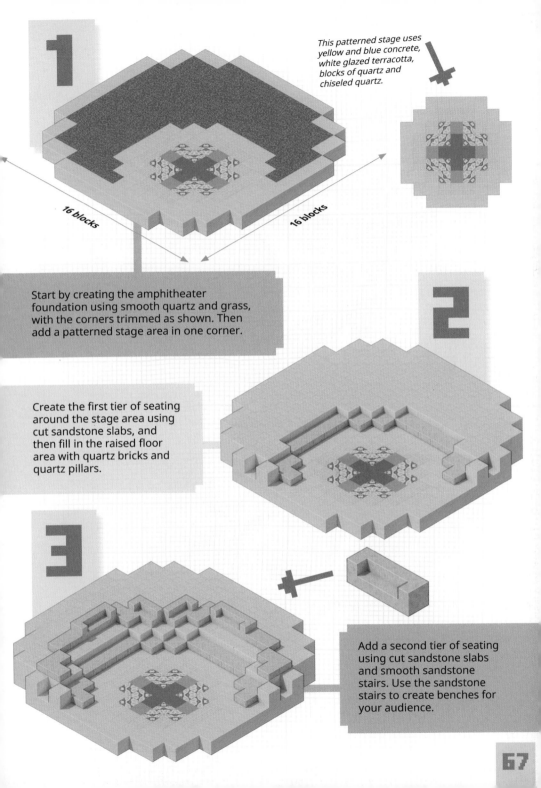

1

This patterned stage uses yellow and blue concrete, white glazed terracotta, blocks of quartz and chiseled quartz.

16 blocks

16 blocks

Start by creating the amphitheater foundation using smooth quartz and grass, with the corners trimmed as shown. Then add a patterned stage area in one corner.

2

Create the first tier of seating around the stage area using cut sandstone slabs, and then fill in the raised floor area with quartz bricks and quartz pillars.

3

Add a second tier of seating using cut sandstone slabs and smooth sandstone stairs. Use the sandstone stairs to create benches for your audience.

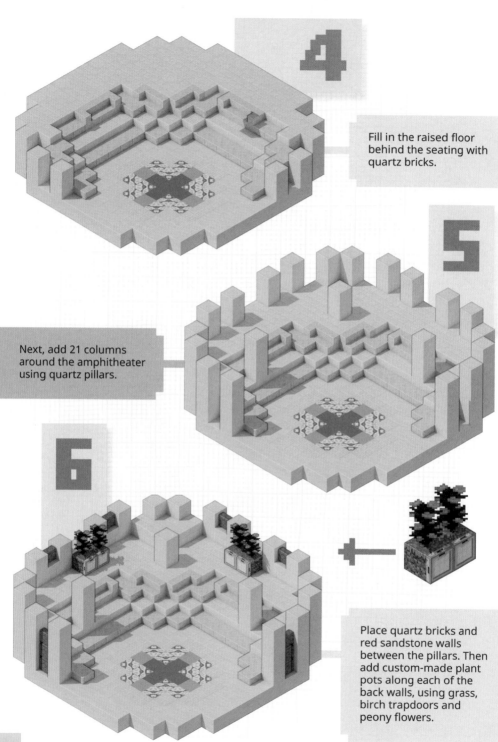

4

Fill in the raised floor behind the seating with quartz bricks.

5

Next, add 21 columns around the amphitheater using quartz pillars.

6

Place quartz bricks and red sandstone walls between the pillars. Then add custom-made plant pots along each of the back walls, using grass, birch trapdoors and peony flowers.

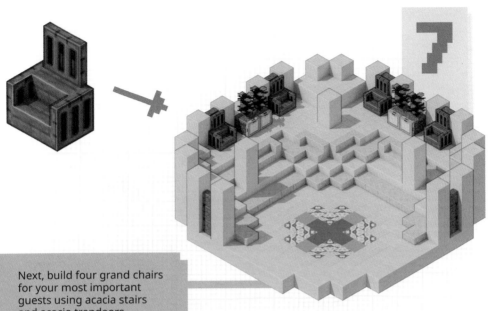

Next, build four grand chairs for your most important guests using acacia stairs and acacia trapdoors.

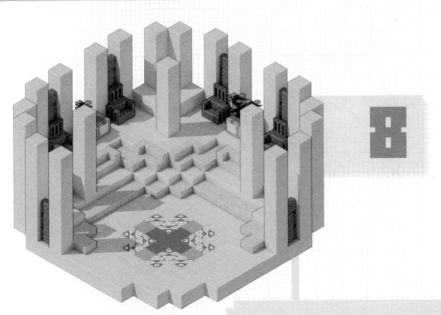

Extend the quartz pillars until they are all at an equal height and place a chiseled quartz block on top of every pillar. Then place more red sandstone walls between the back pillars.

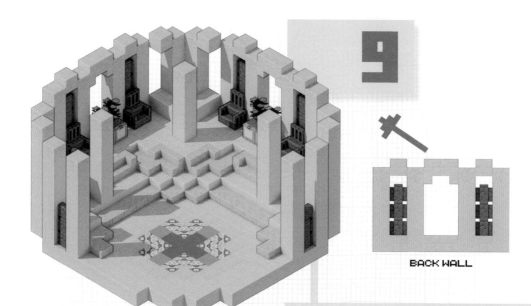

9

BACK WALL

Connect each of the back pillars using smooth quartz slabs and quartz stairs.

You can use the trellis to hang all sorts of decorations, like lanterns!

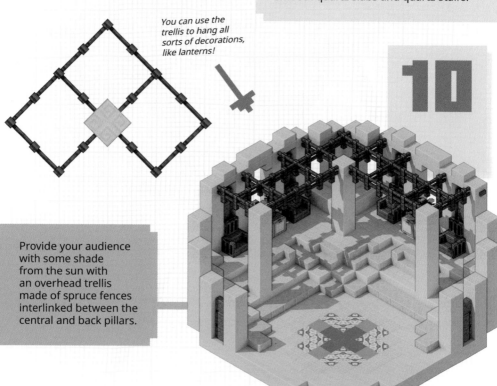

10

Provide your audience with some shade from the sun with an overhead trellis made of spruce fences interlinked between the central and back pillars.

You can also add vines to the sides of the pillars!

Finally, add the finishing touches to make your amphitheater stand out. Put a few campfires around the stage area, cover the overhead trellis with jungle leaves and place acacia buttons at the top of the pillars. It's time to start the show!

STAGE AREAS

You can decorate your stage however you like! This patterned stage uses pink concrete and pink glazed terracotta for a vibrant effect.

This stage area is illuminated with glowstone and orange concrete like a disco dance floor. Perfect for a party!

HIDDEN BUNKER

A great tactic for keeping your base secure is to keep it hidden. Hiding in plain sight will keep prying eyes away. This base is completely invisible from the outside – until you flick a hidden lever to reveal the entrance.

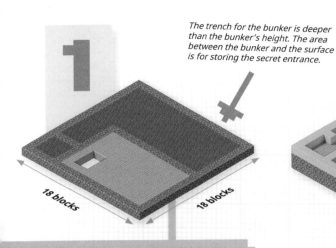

The trench for the bunker is deeper than the bunker's height. The area between the bunker and the surface is for storing the secret entrance.

1

18 blocks
18 blocks

Start by digging a 12-block-deep hole directly into the ground and excavate a 7-block-tall, 18x18 square chamber for the bunker. Then, inside the chamber, create the bunker foundation using cobblestone, stone and birch planks.

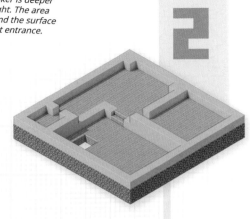

2

Begin building the walls with a layer of cobblestone followed by a layer of white concrete. Then create a raised second-floor level using birch planks and birch stairs.

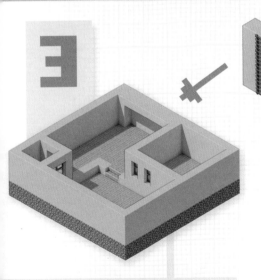

3

Extend the white concrete walls another three blocks, leaving space for doorways, windows and an alcove in the back corner. Place glass panes in the window spaces. In the small room, build a ladder to the ceiling. This is the entrance to the bunker.

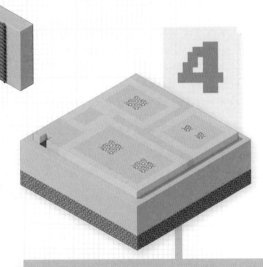

4

Add a stylish ceiling to the bunker using white concrete, glowstone and upside-down smooth quartz stairs. Leave a gap above the ladder to get in and out.

SECRET ENTRANCE

Once you've completed the bunker, it's time to create the secret entrance. Step outside your bunker and dig a 5-block-deep trench above the entrance as shown.

1

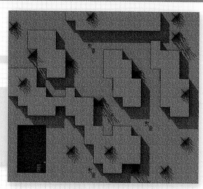

OUTSIDE TOP VIEW

2

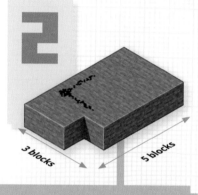

3 blocks

5 blocks

At the bottom of the trench, create a stone platform and place three redstone dust as shown.

3

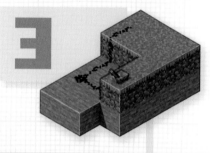

Add eight grass blocks, a lever and a redstone dust on top of the stone platform.

4

Add seven lime terracotta, four redstone dust and a redstone repeater.

5

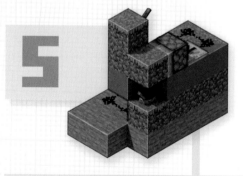

Place a sticky piston in front of the redstone repeater. Then add three more grass blocks and another lever.

6

Next, step inside the bunker and extend the ladder to reach the grass surface.

7

Finally, disguise the secret entrance and hide the lever using grass. The lever will activate the sticky piston to hide and reveal the entrance to the secret bunker. Make sure the lever is accessible but also hidden from view.

HIDDEN LADDER

When the sticky piston is extended, the entrance is hidden from view.

When the sticky piston is retracted, the entrance becomes visible.

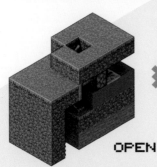

OPEN

CLOSED

HOUSEHOLD ESSENTIALS

Next, fill your hidden bunker with all the household essentials. This bunker has three main rooms: a kitchen, a bedroom and a lobby.

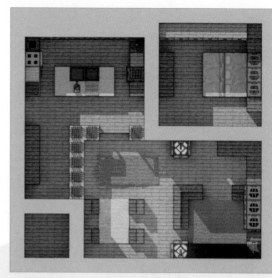

FLOOR PLAN

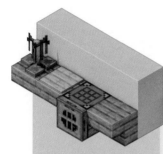

Equip the kitchen with some survival essentials, like a crafting table and brewing stand.

Create a shelving unit using jungle stairs, slabs and trapdoors. You can also add a flower in a flower pot.

Build a large wardrobe using birch doors, birch trapdoors and birch slabs.

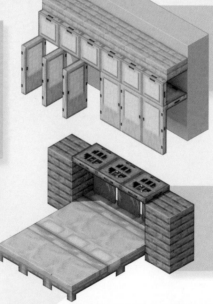

Make a queen-size bed using jungle planks, jungle trapdoors, banners and beds.

Create a modern fridge for your bunker with an iron block, iron door, trapdoor and stone button. Place a chest full of food in the fridge, and some smokers nearby to cook the food.

Use smooth quartz stairs, water cauldrons, a lever and a pressure plate to create a kitchen counter.

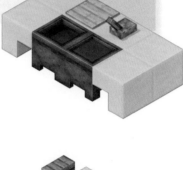

Add a decorative storage area in the kitchen using jungle stairs and trapdoors, chests, glowstones and furnace-and-rail stoves.

Create a dining table using redstone torches and sticky pistons. Dig a space for the redstone torches below the sticky pistons, then use carpets as a table cloth and jungle stairs for seating.

Build a TV set using jungle stairs, jungle slabs, black concrete and a painting. Add extra detail with a redstone lamp and lever light, and a large fern in a custom-made plant pot.

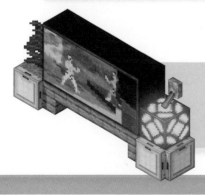

DOLPHIN FOUNTAIN

Dolphins are social creatures that love to interact with players. Brighten up the day for everyone in town with this special water fountain. This build will use lots of prismarine to create a lifelike dolphin statue.

DIFFICULTY:
★★☆☆☆
🕐 20 mins

BUILD TIP

Keep the fountain at surface level by placing the quartz and prismarine base in a 1-block-deep trench.

11 blocks

Prismarine bricks

7 blocks

5 blocks

Prismarine brick slab

Prismarine brick stairs

Prismarine slab

Quartz stairs

6 blocks

Dark prismarine slab

5 blocks

Dark prismarine

Prismarine

Stone bricks

Stone

Chiseled stone

Quartz

15 blocks

15 blocks

Dirt

79

AVIARY PYRAMID

This glassy geometric marvel is complete with a custom-made tree and perches for your feathered friends. Pyramids are strong structures with four cascading sides around a square base. Though they look impressive, they're deceptively easy to build.

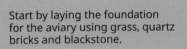

Start by laying the foundation for the aviary using grass, quartz bricks and blackstone.

14 blocks

16 blocks

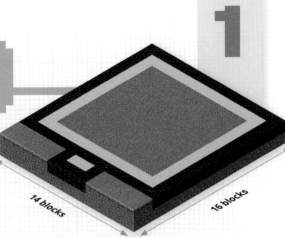

Build a 2-block-tall wall around the foundation using polished blackstone bricks and orange stained glass.

Then, using the same blocks, create a ring that's one block narrower around the foundation walls.

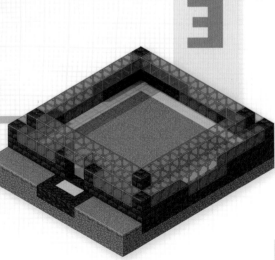

4

Add another ring, one block narrower, using polished blackstone and polished blackstone stairs.

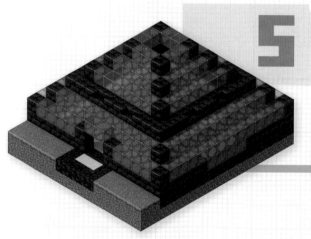

5

Continue adding three more rings of polished blackstone bricks and orange stained glass to the pyramid, each ring narrower than the last.

6

Complete the pyramid with a chiseled polished blackstone roof. Then place two birch doors at the entrance to the pyramid.

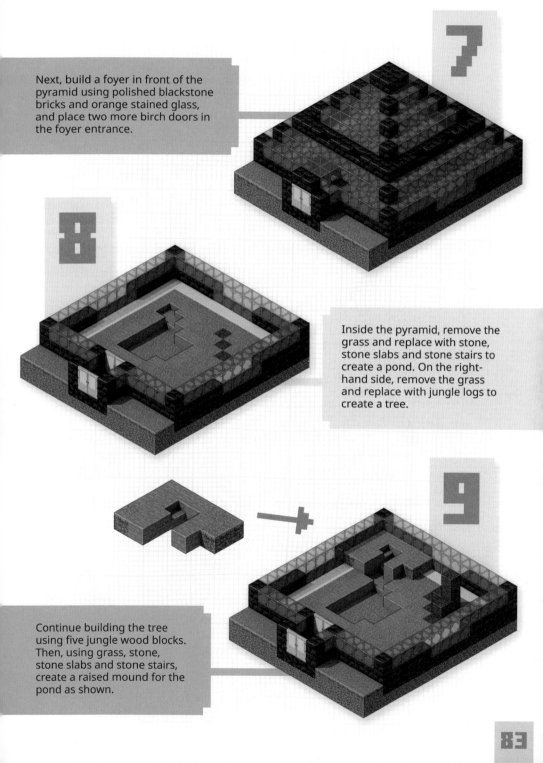

Next, build a foyer in front of the pyramid using polished blackstone bricks and orange stained glass, and place two more birch doors in the foyer entrance.

7

8

Inside the pyramid, remove the grass and replace with stone, stone slabs and stone stairs to create a pond. On the right-hand side, remove the grass and replace with jungle logs to create a tree.

9

Continue building the tree using five jungle wood blocks. Then, using grass, stone, stone slabs and stone stairs, create a raised mound for the pond as shown.

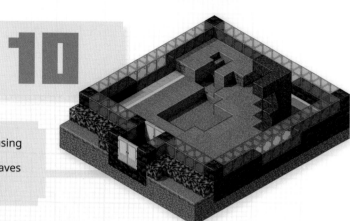

Add branches to the tree using another five jungle wood blocks, and place jungle leaves by the entrance.

Add two more branches to the tree using jungle wood as shown, and add another two branches jutting out from the new branches.

PERCH

Next, create perches for the birds of the aviary with six jungle fences placed against the tree.

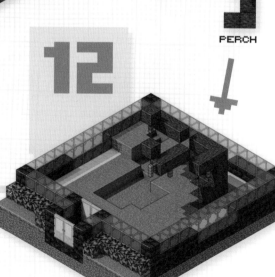

13

Add jungle leaves to the branches to complete the tree.

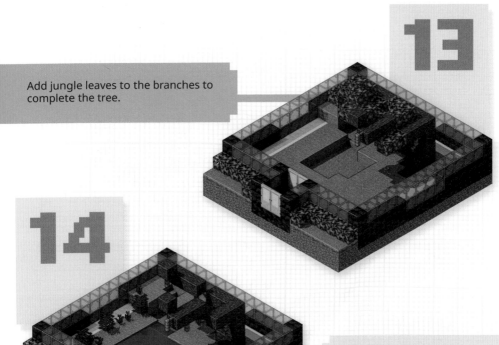

14

Fill the pond with water buckets and then place ferns and flowers around the build.

15

Finally, add parrots inside the pyramid to complete the aviary. Make sure you keep the doors closed to keep the parrots safely inside!

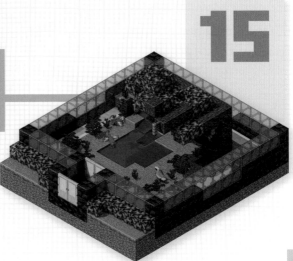

DEEP-SEA SUBMARINE

There's an entire world hidden beneath the ocean, and what better way to see it than with your own private submarine. To complete this aquatic build, you'll need to wrangle with some unique underwater construction problems, like placing redstone and draining water.

DIFFICULTY:
★★★★★
🕐 35 mins

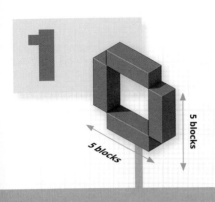

1

Start by creating the circular shape of the submarine hull using light gray concrete.

5 blocks

5 blocks

2

Extend the submarine hull into a 9-block-long cylindrical shape, keeping a 2-block gap in the center.

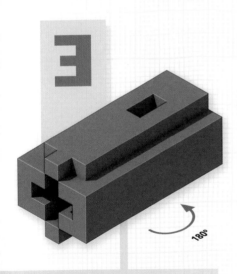

3

180°

At the back of the hull, add a wall of light gray concrete leaving a +-shaped gap.

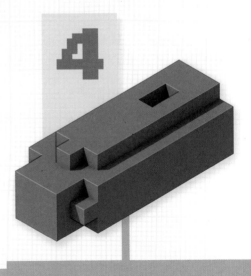

4

Add two more walls of light gray concrete to the back of the hull.

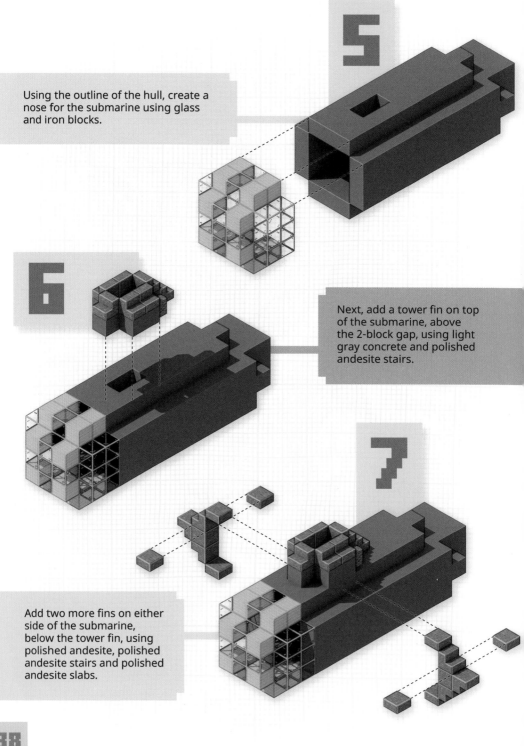

5

Using the outline of the hull, create a nose for the submarine using glass and iron blocks.

6

Next, add a tower fin on top of the submarine, above the 2-block gap, using light gray concrete and polished andesite stairs.

7

Add two more fins on either side of the submarine, below the tower fin, using polished andesite, polished andesite stairs and polished andesite slabs.

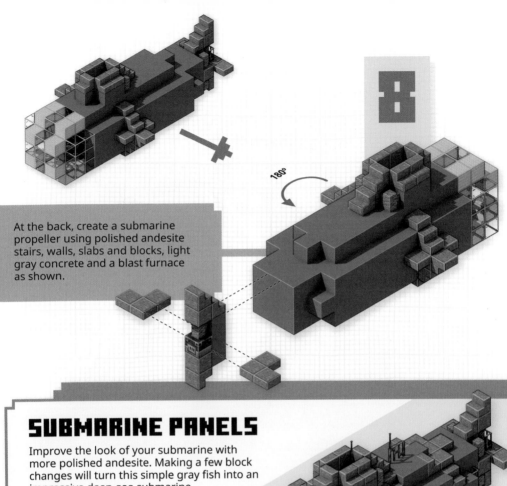

At the back, create a submarine propeller using polished andesite stairs, walls, slabs and blocks, light gray concrete and a blast furnace as shown.

180°

SUBMARINE PANELS

Improve the look of your submarine with more polished andesite. Making a few block changes will turn this simple gray fish into an impressive deep-sea submarine.

Remove and replace the light gray concrete around the fins with polished andesite stairs and glass blocks.

Add more polished andesite slabs and stairs at the rear of the submarine.

UNDERWATER AIRLOCK

Underwater structures have two major threats: flooding and drowned mobs. You can rid yourself of one of those problems by building an airlock. With an airlock, you will be able to get in and out of any submerged structure without any risk of flooding.

BUILD TIP

Redstone dust cannot be placed underwater. Before starting, create an air bubble around the airlock using temporary blocks and sponges. When you're finished, remove the temporary blocks.

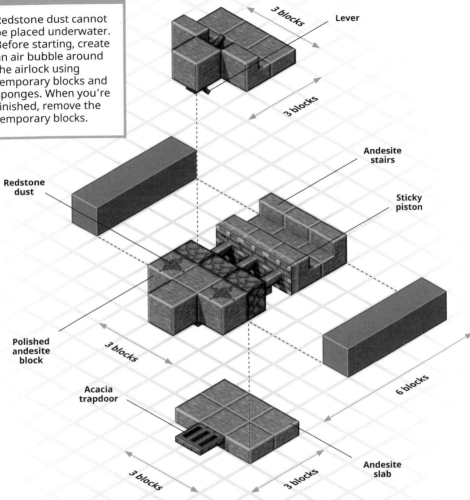

Lever

3 blocks

3 blocks

Andesite stairs

Sticky piston

Redstone dust

Polished andesite block

3 blocks

6 blocks

Acacia trapdoor

3 blocks

3 blocks

Andesite slab

REDSTONE MECHANISM

This airlock is designed to fit directly to the underside of the deep-sea explorer in the previous build. Simply flick the lever to open the trapdoor and climb in! The trapdoor will automatically close behind you.

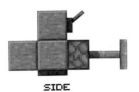

SIDE

BOTTOM

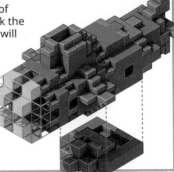

COMBINATION CHALLENGES

If you've made it this far, congratulations! You must be quite the builder. But you're not done yet! The guides in this book have covered a lot of invaluable building skills and we want you to put your skills to the test.

Listed below are a series of combination challenges. For each of these challenges, we want you to combine the builds using the guides and build tips included in this book. How you combine the builds is completely up to you: you can resize the builds, pick new blocks or improve the design as you see fit.

1 HALLOWEEN MAZE + CREEPER

Create a maze with a creeper centerpiece.

2 FOUNTAIN + BIRD AVIARY

Merge the fountain and bird aviary into one build.

3 TRAIN STATION + CART DISPENSER

Create a transport system with multiple stops.

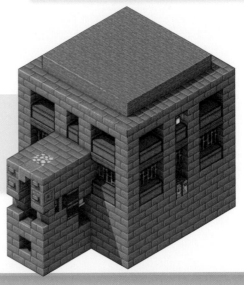

4 ITEM DESTROYER + HIDDEN BUNKER

Build a hidden bunker with a built-in item destroyer.

5 VAULT + ALARM SYSTEM

Add an extra layer of security to your vault with an alarm system.

GOODBYE

And there we have it! We've traversed the skies, dived deep below the ocean and safeguarded the Overworld from potential Nether invasions. And as the sun went down, we retired to a beach house to watch the sunset.

The fun doesn't stop here! Each of these builds teaches some core skills that can be used, adapted and repeated in many ways. We hope you've learned some new tricks while completing the builds and that they have inspired you to create new structures and develop old ones. We can't wait to see what you will create using the new knowledge you've accrued.

Remember, there's no right or wrong way to create in Minecraft. This is your game, and you are the master of your world. So until next time, keep crafting, creating and developing. Embrace your creativity, follow your instinct and have fun!

JOURNEY INTO THE WORLD OF

—BOOKS FOR EVERY READING LEVEL—

OFFICIAL NOVELS:

FOR YOUNGER READERS:

OFFICIAL GUIDES:

DISCOVER MORE AT READMINECRAFT.COM

Penguin
Random
House